Inspirations

Inspirations
Majestic Forte
Marcus Yates Ford

Copyright © 2018 Marcus Yates Ford
Majestic Forte All rights reserved. No part of this book may be reproduced, stored in a retrieval system or transmitted in any form or by any means without the prior written permission of the publishers, except by reviewer who may quote brief passages in a review to be printed in a newspaper, magazine, or journal

ISBN-13: 9780692143292
ISBN-10: 0692143297
Published by: Majestic Forte
The MF Signature
Houston, Texas

Printed in the United States

Dedication

To The Spirit that drives me to help others and
continue to spread HIS word

Inspirations

Inspired by

I said one more book and I am finished
However, let us say this is a revision, better yet,
An extension of the last chapter
More of a reflection on the spiritual
As my mind flows with the Spirit
Time after time, I changed my mind,
But I finally released HIS intentions

Inspirations

Poems, Prayers & Perspectives

-Prelude: The Pulpit

-Rose

-Victory

-Name Above All Names

-The Connection in the Clouds

-Who am I

-Where I'm From

-This is your Life

-I Choose

-Belief

-Trends and Blends

-The Lamp

-Celebrate

-Walk through my Thoughts…4/4 passport

-Dreams, Miracles, and Victory

-Coin Number 21:22

-Your Part

-Direction

-Process

-Community

- May Peace be with you
- The Path / (Revision)
- PHLI Prayer
- Jubilee
- Trouble Man
- A Connoisseur's Limited Release
- Alone
- My S.O.S to the World
- Inspired from a Song/Playlist of the Songs
- Emotions of a Sinner
- Daily
- The Defining Moment
- Legacy
- Imagine
- The List
- A Billion Smiles Message
- Reflection
- Pin
- Grace, Mercy, and Love
- Reflections of Works: Epilogue

The Prelude: The Pulpit

I'm a poetic writer not a poetic reciter,
I'm not here to entertain the crowd
This is my therapy, which keeps me on the ground
The reward I seek
Is when YOU speak my name in the Book of Life
I know I have done plenty of wrong
However, my heart wants to do plenty of right
I repent of my sins
I will use Freedom of the Mind; the open mic,
To spread Your Word and shed Your light
I will speak the truth; I can't make it without YOU
Give me the strength; be by my side
As I deliver the words that I wrote down
Let them reach like the Sermon on the Mount
It's about the mind, the pen, and the paper
That will show the reflections of my soul
It's time to be bold,
My legacy is to live in the streets of gold
Therefore, I will use Love, Grace and Imani
As part of the journey to Discover Devotion
It was YOU that saved me from the ocean;
More accurately the Caribbean Sea
Through Your teachings, it brought me peace
Speak to my heart so I can be the best version of me
Let me accomplish my goals
Directed by YOU piece by piece
Inspirations from God, the 5th book We released

Colossians 3:23

Rose

When I first rose out of the water
I said oh that is my King
The Light Shining that magical beam
The most beautiful thing I have ever seen
I'm a new being, I've been renewed
The courage to repent of my old ways
The blood covered me;
YOU found me
And walked with me on my new journey
Which is to stay strong and witness to the world
what I believe…
YOU are the Savior and that is all I need.

2 Corinthians 5:17

Victory

When you first opened up your eyes,
I said they look so familiar
Like I have been looking at them for a lifetime.
My baby girl, I am mesmerized
As I stare like what a wonder...
Tears flow inside of me
And I pray for a lifetime with you...
God's WORD is so true,
So I must dedicate you back to HIM,
I have to trust HIM with you...
HE brought me this far,
What a miracle to see, a Victory, for us,
I pray that you only have the best from us,
You are our miracle, all the things we never knew,
You are our miracle look at what GOD can do,
HE made us a perfect you,
We pray for you to accomplish all of your dreams
and to enjoy the world we brought you into,
And with joyful cares and humble hearts,
We will always love you

Jeremiah 1:5Psalms 127:3

Name Above All Names

I will have the courage
To proclaim the name above all of names
There is No other name that can heal me
There is No other name that can give me vision
There is No other name that can give me joy
There is No other name that can give me wisdom

There is No other name
that can bring me out of darkness
There is No other name
that can put me on the path of righteousness
There is No other name that can forgive me
There is No other name that can take me higher
There is No other name
that can give me the truth and light
There is No other name
that can show me what is right
There is No other name that is there when I call
There is No other name that is there when I fall
There is No other name that speaks to my heart
There is No other name
that can put me together when I'm apart
There is No other name that is light as a feather
There is No other name that can change the weather
There is No other name that can make me better
There is No other name that can quench my thirst
I will have courage to put the Messiah first
There is only one name "Jesus"

Philippians 2:9

The Connection in the Clouds

As I connect to the clouds,
My mind connects to YOU,
I think of how close YOU are
But YOU are visibly so far,
That magical plane ride
That makes me reflect each time,
That perfect peace of reflection,
YOU become closer and closer, speak to my heart,
right here, right now, show me Your ways,
Show me the direction YOU want me to go,
My destination is to be Your follower,
A lifetime of smiles, I know it took a while
But each time in the sky,
I always felt YOU by my side,
Even on land, YOU are my guide,
I need to stay focused on the Spirit YOU left for me
And to let Your ways dominate my thoughts...
Love, faith and hope....
Bring that drive to complete my calling.
As I look at the clouds,
I realize I'm blessed to be an instrument
That YOU use for Your purpose,
That energy that is unexplainable,
Trusting and believing the process of
Joy for the journey
I accepted I'm Your child, following instructions of
Your plan

Who am I

Who is HE, if it wasn't for the Blood
Who am I, one of the children
From the ALL Mighty LORD
Who am I, a human here to express thoughts of love
Who is HE, the SON sent from heaven above
Who am I, the one to share the Christian Experience
Who am I, the one trusting Jesus for deliverance
HE is the reason I stand and I'm breathing
Who am I, the person that stands for forgiveness
and the cleansing of the soul
Who am I,
The one that made it through the fire and the cold
Who am I, a person that lets
The Spirit borrow this body to teach
The one that practices the ritual,
Now let us break this bread and eat
HE is the one
Who wipes away the tears from those who weep,
Drink this wine for it is My blood,
And do this in remembrance of Me
It is I you seek
Who is HE, the one that takes the weak
And restores them to their peak
Who is HE,
The one you should fall to and wash His feet
The ONE when it is all over you want to hear say
"Well Done"
Now everything is perfect and complete
Who am I, a child of God, it's righteousness I seek

1 John 4:15

Where I'm From

Where I'm from,
God's grace has allowed me to see the SON,
All I did is ask for it to come
And with the WORD it brought greatness with a
foundation that is as solid as a rock.
It was built piece by piece
With victories and struggles…
HIS WILL will be done; I stand a product of faith,
That's where I'm from.
Living with blessings, another day has begun…
As reflected on the teachings
And the messages that gave me
The strength to know HE was in reach,
That WORD that helps me rise from defeat.
The light in the dark, which allows me to see,
The connection of prayers
Which allows HIM to speak,
So I remain still and know HE is LORD…
The Anchor and captain of this ship,
I'm all aboard…
The entry of God's Child…
Mr. Marcus Yates Ford

This is your Life

As I reflect on where I have been or better yet
where YOU have taken me
I am still amazed at how much YOU Love me
The path of destruction I embraced
The scars that show the trace of the mistakes
But the stories I'm able to tell
Because YOU brought me through...
When I was alone it was only YOU,
YOU lifted me,
YOU took care of me,
YOU helped me escape,
YOU saved me,
YOU healed me,
YOU comforted me...
Now I can only attempt to show my gratitude
By speaking Your name, Explaining to others how
YOU brought me through the storms....
The sunshine is a testimony of the victory,
LORD thank YOU
For the new blessings YOU have put in my life,
I never dreamed of this life,
That I'm somebody's husband and father,
That I'm the spiritual leader for
My child and my wife...
Your WILL has brought me through
And this is just the beginning

2 Timothy 1:8-12

I Choose

I choose to love
Because it heals
I choose to focus on the present
Because I cannot change the past
I choose to forgive
Because it is the only way for me to live
I choose to have hope
Because it carries me to places of purity
I choose to express joy
Because it is inside me,
Given to me by the GodHead
I choose to be thankful
Because I realize things could be worse
I choose to be humble
Because I see I am here by grace
I choose to help
Because I am in touch with sympathy and empathy
I choose to listen
Because it is what completes me
I choose to travel light
With the essentials of love, hope and faith
Because that is all I need at any destination
Or in any situation

I Choose

(Inspirations: Prayer)

Dear God, grant me the peace in my heart not to worry and lose the need to control. Let me trust in YOU through my actions. Give me the peace in my mind that YOU are working out all of my concerns. I ask for continual covering for my loved ones. Help me to develop the faith to know that everything will be okay. Let me not focus on what can be seen but focus on the unseen. Thank you for protection and the opportunity to see Your signs, miracles and wonders. Continue to mold me, in Jesus' Name, Amen.

Belief

No need for an idol, never become idle
Stay bold even when it is cold
Advance forward… reach your goal
No calf of gold, stay focused on the scriptures to protect us from our downfall
What is our call?
To share the WORD, the mobility to use the gifts
God has given me, trust my ability?
Use the testimony to connect the humility that a blessing came from YOU
Like the gospel song "What do you do"
when times are hard I look to YOU,
I reflect on Your goodness, I share Your goodness,
I lean on Your goodness
I believe

John 14:12

Trends and Blends

No need to hide or to blend
It's HIS image, HIS Mission
I have been called into action
Same WORD
I am just communicating through style and passion
New look, new fashion
Robins Jeans, displays Angel Wings to the masses
Savior and Stars
Is what my necklace is trying to capture
That is what I am marketing,
Certain trends connect I'm aware
American dreaming,
But Heaven focused is the where
Let us blend
This is the market,
Is this what I want to pursue?
I need to stay focused on Matthew 22
Verse 37 to be exact
Verse 39 I want to market that
That human love so they can see the TRUTH
It is the conversation
And another way to display YOU
Truly, golden...let the gold glisten
It is HIS image, HIS mission

Matthew 4:19

The Lamp

If this is called Poetry
Then I have been writing ever since '81,
When I picked up Silverstein, *A Light in the Attic*
I have been writing since I was five,
Now that is mathematic,
Very enlightened, go purchase *A Light in the Attic*
Because it's a light in this attic
That shines bright enough to generate electricity
Touch this man and feel this static
My knowledge is shocking like thunder
It is lighting when I start to wonder
Brainstorming is upon us,
December of '75
They would lie to create a gift,
9/10/76
I would arrive,
Better known as the prince
The scion,
Your majesty,
Majestic Forte the blueprint
The scroll,
A connection to the KEY
Give me the courage
To be who YOU called me to be
A disciple of Christ…

Matthew 5:14-16

The Lamp

(Inspirations: Prayer)

Thank you LORD for waking me up this morning, thank you for this Super Bowl Sunday, this super bowl we are in, the bowl which is the sanctuary, where Your super presence is, thank you for Your grace and mercy, let us hear a Word from YOU, let Jesus take over our temple and let the Holy Spirit guide our actions, Lord please forgive this sinner and let me have a new start and continue to improve so I can spread Your word, YOU are so good to me, YOU are better than good, YOU are the best thing that ever happened to me....

I need Your power in Jesus' Name, Amen

Celebrate

As I enjoy Rose' Champagne
Because HE took the pain,
We can have eternal life,
I keep that in sight,
God be to the Glory that I write,
So let us celebrate day and night,
Father forgive me of my sins,
Turn water into wine in my life,
Elevate me to a greater mindset,
One that displays Your glory,
Let me communicate,
Your story, Your WILL, Your greatness,
Give me the courage to show my Christian
Experience through my walk,
Therefore, I raise this flute because
Acknowledgment is a good start,
Only let love be displayed in my heart,
Show me the chart to my path,
Here's to Life, let us raise our glass

Ecclesiastes 9:7

Walk through My Thoughts... 4/4 passport

I knew I wanted to know your name
And when that opportunity came,
My life would not be the same,
As I dreamed of those freckles on your face,
My prayers would be answered in another place,
now we are both in a space, so let me speak.
I finally got some time away
From the life everyone wanted,
All I ever wanted was to come home to you like
Babyface in the 90s,
I finally got that life,
I love the way we pray each morning,
I love the way God is opening the doors
I have always dreamed of,
No one else that I would dedicate my life too,
I always knew it was you,
It was just a storm I had to go through,
To know HE is the truth, the rock, the foundation,
My strength to hold us,
Holding us up to expectations,
The love, the patience, the way we embrace,
4/4 is here again and I'm so glad,
I did something right, your smile and laugh
Nothing else comforts me like those expression,
I just want to tell you I love the way you love

It's time to set the bar, we've come this far,
The stars at night
Let's make it right
It's April 4th,
The day that brings so much anticipation

Walk through My Thoughts... continued

My heart's implications, knowing God's smiling as
I choose the direction HE puts in my path
I'm here at last,
Here's to the future as we pass our past
I drop my mask, you I want much more
Here we are April 4th, you I adore
Let me adorn, as the doves soar,
Holy Spirit from the Lord
Puts me on course, all aboard, just me and you
April 4th, we hold hands and now we are on course
We travel the globe, the blue waters,
The plane rides, the matching rings
As I hear you sing, Lord speak to my heart,
My Love, you have me for the rest of your life
Husband and wife, husband and wife,
Yes I said it twice
Because its so nice, to the top of the peak,
Let's reach new heights
Where we cannot see the floor
My mind on replay of April 4th
The penthouse suite, you're too sweet
Just you and me,
Now you see that dreams come true
The Spirit reigning in me, listening to my calling
The courage to do what HE wants me to do
Witness to the world, save souls;
Share His love with you by my side
The beauty of life and there is so much more
It's April 4th, yes it's April 4th

Dreams, Miracles, and Victory

Thank you Lord for waking me up.
I thank you for the doors
YOU have opened for me...
I am not alone anymore;
I see the blessings that I share,
I see she is right here; we are family,
Now protect us and give us the courage
As we expand, give us Victory,
Give us strength and knowledge
To endure the journey and provide endless joy,
This miracle we give back to YOU
And Your Word we share,
We will teach Your Love,
We will show how hope
And faith carry us beyond our understanding,
We are on solid ground, Your solid landing,
Your impenetrable foundation,
The Tree of Life,
The Branches connecting us to a prosperous display
that shows all of Your grace and mercy,
YOU are bringing all of the dreams we never knew,
The dream that keeps giving us more and more,
Now it is so clear and with so much clarity,
The answer is Your WILL
Thank you for the miracle

Coin Number 21:22

Now sturdy and straight,
We are not concerned with faith
Because you continue to seek
And you do not want to patiently wait
Someone's ruins is another's treasure
Some never took the time to measure
All of us just flipping coins into the well
Quarters, dimes, nickels and pennies just stack
However, they all have a story to tell
Listen to the wind at the fountain
They tell about the lost dreams
That people thought those coins could make
Dreams come and go!
However, dreams continue to create
Sometimes dreams do not occur
Because the dreamers dream too late
On the other hand,
Maybe the order of operations was misplaced
'And whatever things you ask in prayer,
Believing, you will receive"
This is where dreams are conceived
This is how dreams are achieved

Your Part

Love has brought me closer to YOU
Love has brought me smiles
Love has brought me tears of joy

Love has cured my hurt
Love has caused me to feel my heart is whole again

Love has made me a better person
Love has made me analyze situations
Love has made me forgive my neighbor
Love has allowed me to try again

Love has brought me close to The Highest,
There is no Better Friend
Thank you for loving me despite my faults
Thank you for loving the deepness of my heart
And not my quick thoughts
Thank you for your patience
That I am worthy enough to be taught

John 15:13

I remember

I remember when YOU would not give up on me
I remember when I was lonely and sad
I remember when I thought about the pain and past
I remember when an hour felt like a lifetime
I remember when I had too much pride
I remember when I would not let love guide
I remember when I wouldn't let my heart hurt again
I remember when I came back
I remember when I became worry free
I remember when I could not let go
I remember when
YOU said YOU would make me whole again
I remember when
YOU would accept me back every time I left
My energy continues to think GOD vibes;
I continue to live with unconditional love,
Great words and beautiful thoughts,
Every time I am so far, that message is so clear,
That YOU are always near
I continue to grow into a better person.
Dreams continue to surround my presence
And the joys of pleasure filter
into my streams of happiness,
My state of mind, the gears moving so smooth,
Now it's so clear,
What I once feared is what makes me cheer
I will never be lonely because I am not alone,
YOU are always right here in my heart
Accepting Christ is the start
Now, Holy Spirit guide me
Romans 15:13

Direction

You can't give up now because of how you feel
HE sacrificed to give you the courage
To endure the trial and whatever comes your way
Therefore, whatever you are going through, ask the
Spirit to connect and take you to safety
HE always cares so go to HIM Night or Day
HE's always there and so much more
HE will teach you to grow free from this World,
HE will give you His Word
Bring you to the lightness, HE is above
Darkness has no power over you,
So take that step towards empowerment
And you won't have to worry about how you feel,
You will have the protection of the seal,
The seal of truth, It's that time to renew,
I'm a living witness HE will see you through.

1 John 4:4

Process

It takes courage to trust the process,
The process that HE is in control of,
Now is not the time to question,
Must stand bold and declare I accept this path,
This journey,
I am willing to learn so I can teach,
My testimony will be about the feat,
And how doubt ensured defeat,
Therefore, I rise to my feet and
Accomplish what is known as peace,
Peace of mind that HE is in control
And I will serve to make my mission complete.
Good works is my path

Ephesians 2:10

Community

To the community that raised me,
As time moves forward
I look back in the previous chapters of this life
Mama laid down the foundation
And gardened the soil
It was Barbara Jean
People can thank for me being spoiled
My God Mother passed away July 2017
Within 48 hours of My Aunt Helen
The lady who taught me about diamonds and gold
She loved to cook me pork chops on the burner
Stevie Wonder said it best,
I never dreamed you'd leave in summer
I often ponder how you two loved me like your own
The deposits that helped me become grown
The love that is in me, you two are not alone
I shed a quick tear
Because I know you two are home
I'm happy for the memories, more enjoyable
moments are on pause, they have been postponed
So with that being said
Dear Mama, Thank you for sharing me
And letting others impact my life
I want you to know how you inspired me
And how things took flight
From the first day, I saw your face,
The gift from God; we embrace
From the days you fed me by spoon,
From the day you gave me a room
From the day you taught me about the stars
And the moon

Community continued

How you taught me about the Son
And HE made the Sun and the sky blue
You let me know I am here for a purpose
And always stay true
You motivate me in the Spring, the Summer,
the Fall, the Winter; the four seasons
When I was in Lanai at the Four Seasons,
I told myself this is the reason
I saw you travel
And take those adventures that sparked my interests
You were the model before *Pinterest*
What more can I say about you?
You are the definition of love
You are kind and patient
I thank God that you were able to see me
grow and mature
Your lessons were not in vain,
I admire the way you show strength
When there was pain
I know losing your son in 2012,
Things will never be the same
I see how you contribute to the Bereavement
Ministry at the church
You are always thinking of others
There is not enough paper to write about
You being an outstanding mother
My greatest gift God allowed me
to give you came in 2017 September,
Now you have granddaughter
I enjoy sitting back watching you two play together,

Community continued

This is just a small testament
To let you know how I feel
I love you forever, I always will, nothing pleases
me more how we continue to grow in God's Will
What a blessing to have you, Inspirations

May Peace be with you

If the good die young and we get better with age
The best potential has been buried
But their soul has been saved

A tombstone message at their grave
Alternative version
Let their ashes be scattered among the waves

I see the pain in their face; their tears flow with ease
I pray you didn't absorb their pain in their transition
I pray you were at peace and listening to the
Angels' whispers
Joy for the Journey, time for the next adventure

As long as I breathe, you breathe
As long as I laugh, you laugh
As long as I smile, you smile
Lives you have touched,
Those will be the thoughts among them and us:

Rest in peace for all the ones we have lost
Wear your crown

May Peace be with you

(Inspirations: Prayer)

It's me again, LORD thank you that I can pray any time of the day and for how long... Pray for thanksgiving, Pray for the storm that we are in: parents who have lost children, children who have lost parents, siblings who have lost siblings, nephews/nieces who have lost uncles and aunts, uncles and aunts who have lost nephews and nieces, family members who have lost family, friends who have lost friends, thank you for the endless and great memories of those individuals, Lord so I leave all of my concerns and pain with YOU and bow before YOU...just say the word and we are healed, I know YOU can heal us, thank you for being our rock; our foundation, in Jesus' Name, Amen

The Path

I made mistakes,
I ran away from who YOU wanted me to become
Therefore, what do I have to say to YOU;
Yes, I am still a work in progress
I see who YOU want me to be,
Give me the strength to conquer

I will not give up; I want to achieve my calling
Give me another chance; it is time to stand
Thank you for being right by my side, yes;
YOU are so good my ultimate guide
I will survive; time to put this plan in drive

This is how courage begins,
YOU are more than my Savior,
YOU are my ultimate friend,
There is no one that can love me like YOU,
Chance after chance YOU spare my faults,
I repent and pray for change,
I know it's the Word I must use against the World,
when it comes to me

YOU never give up,
YOU never give up,
YOU never give up,
Continue to give me the courage
To conquer my short comings

The Path (Revision)

This is how courage begins,
YOU are more than my Savior,
YOU are my ultimate friend,
There is no one that can love me like YOU,
Chance after chance YOU spare my faults,
I repent and pray for change,
I know it's the Word I must use against the World,
when it comes to me

I made mistakes,
I ran away from who YOU wanted me to become
So what do I have to say,
Yes I'm still a work in progress
I see who YOU want me to be,
Give me the strength to conquer

I'll never give up,
I'll never give up,
I'll never give up,
Continue to give me the courage
To conquer my shortcomings

I will not give up; I want to achieve my calling
Give me another chance; it is time to stand
Thank you for being right by my side,
Yes, You're so good; my ultimate guide
I will survive; time to put this plan in drive...
Tears of joy

PHLI Prayer

Dear LORD let everything that has breath praise YOU, we praise YOU for the storms, we praise YOU that we are able to stand on a rock, we praise YOU for Jesus' sacrifice, we praise YOU Jesus that YOU came, we pray that we learn more about that name, we praise YOU for Your wisdom and for teaching us how to pray, we thank YOU for the Holy Spirit, In our new walk let us stay bible accurate, Christ centered, as we execute Matthew 22:39, let us do it with contemporary, creative and cutting edge approach, let us stay PHLI as our mission which is simple "I love helping people" as we know YOU are love, we praise You for every breath, now let us give You every praise!
In Jesus' Name, Amen ....Hallelujah

Jubilee

LORD, I know YOU are always here for us, I know prayer changes things, I know if we ask in your name and if it is Your will, YOU will deliver, Lord I'm not here to ask for anything right at this moment, well I'm asking YOU to listen to something I don't do enough of, I want to give thanks, thank you for covering me, thank for the 52 weeks, The Joyful January, February of Favor, The Magnificent March, The Aspirations of April, Marvelous May, The Joyful June, The Jolly July, The Awesome August, The Sentimental September, The Outstanding October, The Nurturing November, and a Delightful December, thank you for my family, thank you for my brothers and my sisters that you have sent to help me ,thank you for the fathers that continue to father me, thank you for guiding me, thank you for softening my heart, thank you for not allowing my sin to decay me, thank you for Your renewal, thank you for Your Word that strengths me when I'm weak, thank you for Your strength, thank you that when I'm tired, I hear a sweet song from the choir that touches my spirit, thank you for the praise team, choir and band that bring the sound to help enhance my worship experience, thank you for the ministries that let me give more of my time, talent and treasures, Lord thank you for the Word from the pulpit that either convicts me, encourages me or confirms to me that this is what I need to do, thank you for using me despite my shortcomings, and giving me the power

Jubilee continued

of the Holy Spirit to tap into the greatness of YOU, thank you for sharing Your Son and His sacrifice so that I can even stand here and speak with YOU, I can go on for a lifetime thanking you, continue to let me be thankful for every breath, every morning and every opportunity, thank you for all the people that YOU brought into my life for a season or a lifetime to help enhance me, thank you for those teachable moments, thank you for all the reasons to smile, thank you for this year's jubilee, thank you that YOU use all things for good, Lord continue to speak to my heart, I ask all these things in your Son's holy name, Jesus the Redeemer, and all of God's people said Amen

Trouble Man

LORD, I pray for a clean heart, I pray for light in the dark, this is how I need to start to heal and let Your Spirit dominate me, I need all Your fruits to keep my spirit at ease, Your mercy and grace are enough, penetrate those thoughts that don't belong, Lord, show me the way to elevate, the great escape from the threat of my ego, let me give more than I receive, let me stay prayed up and focus on the goodness of Your WORD, let me stay away from the advice of this world, let me leave the secular accomplishments alone and focus on the reward YOU have for me. LORD, keep me focused on Your Path, Your Mission, my Calling....let me complete the success YOU have written out for me, Let me hear YOU clearly and block out any distractions designed to make me come up short, Lord help me focus at CHURCH, let me connect with the Dove and the prayers above, thank you for those prayers that brought me through, Lord, keep me on the path to YOU, this my prayer to YOU....
In Jesus' Name, Amen

Psalm 107:6

A Connoisseur's Limited Release

Are you ready?
Because I'm ready for Ready to open,
Sometimes you just want to go where
Everybody knows your name
We are just ordinary people; we are all the same
Sinners saved by Grace
I am at my new favorite place
Let us order a bottle of champagne,
Let us celebrate life
Pop, fizz, clink
I like to enjoy a Rose'
With the color of an immaculate pink
This is what I call a refreshing drink
Let us put that bottle on ice
As I reflect about me life, I celebrate the Victory
How God made a way,
How he brought me through night
There is joy in the morning,
No more darkness only the Light
My foundation is intact;
Faith has brought me through the storms
Love has brought me through the attacks
Hope has always pushed me ahead
So many tears through the years
Trials and Tribulations
James 1:3
I am thankful for this toast

"Cheers"

Alone

When you feel empty and down
What I have found is the light in dark
When I close my eyes
I search my heart
Because my mind did not want to believe.
Did not want to believe the pain was real,
The life of growing older
And the memories I valued were fading away.
The tears of departure, the physical design of a
father and a brother to be there for me.
I am left to figure this out on my own
However, I am not alone; YOU are here, every
second, every minute, every hour, and every year.
Help me, when you close your eyes at night
And open your heart,
I hope you get closer to the Spirit
The memories of how YOU brought me through
Create a carousel in my mind
With the slow rotation of blessings
Being shown to me
As I glance at the Light House
As I'm swimming in mental waves
I'm waiting for the day where I can be rescued
Where my heart can be put back together
Piece by piece

As I prepare for the test of making it
Through the night
I notice the beautiful cut
That left this gorgeous scar in my life

Alone *continued*

I must flicker the lights fast and slow
Maybe HE will see the Code of Morse
Beyond the clouds
My S.O.S to the world,
Please save our souls
Repair me from a broken heart
With love & prayers I'm asking and hoping
Make me Whole, LORD

Isaiah 41:10   Ephesians 3:16

My S.O.S to the World

The next entry is My S.O.S to the World; I wrote this piece when I was 26 and I decided to release it to inspire a different view of life. I decided to include it to help someone to realize we should think about all of our actions before we do them. We should think about how they affect others as well as ourselves. We only get one life on earth and once it is gone then it is gone, there is no coming back. I learned in church that there will be some temporary problems, it is up to us how we deal with them, and either we will use a temporary solution or a permanent one. The only thing in this world that is permanent is death, and suicide is a permanent solution, where you don't see how you affect others. Suicide is a result of using a permanent solution for a temporary problem. Let us exhaust all temporary solutions before we think of this permanent one. My belief is there is a possibility of infinite solutions when you let Jesus help you. HE is the only permanent solution for whatever you are going through.

My S.O.S to the World

The day I committed suicide, the heavens cried
My soul lost to the burning lake,
No last chance for forgiveness
Before I pull this trigger, I made my decision
No repentance, hell is my sentence
My grandparents cried, made it rain that day
My Mom got the news on the freeway,
My woman going through her day
Like everything is okay
Mom called her with the news
That she had to view her youngest son's body nude
I was discovered by the yard man
In the house I grew up in
I left the door unlocked so he could come in
Life got too tough, too many expectations
Too much anticipation, my feelings racing,
I was in the room pacing
No clothes on because I wanted to leave pure,
No more discussion, I'm sure

Bang!!!!

My S.O.S to the World continued

It rains, my mom's phone rang,
And she had to call Baby and say
"Things aren't the same",
Days later my memorial came
Church filled,
I requested my ashes be buried on a hill
So I can finally be on top of the peak
All my life it was righteousness I seek (sought)
One moment I got weak (this is what I thought)
Now, those who misunderstood realize they love me
They cried so dear; some I haven't talk to in years
So many days I maintained through this struggle,
Pray for this soul that's in trouble
Like 9/11 push away the rubble
Misleading action, I remain in a bubble
I stay away from the facts; my bags are packed
So many tears, I know I was selfish
But no more fears, No more hating peers,
No more movie scripts,
I quit…one shot so quick
My eyes open wide, red and ripped
The author of confusion got his wish
My nightmares are reality, now I wish I didn't click

Save Our Souls
This is a permanent solution for a temporary problem; we should always think about the people we will hurt in the process, love heals all wounds.

John 10:10

Inspired from a Song

I know YOU have seen all of things in my life
I have the feeling this can't be life
Even through my vicissitudes,
I know YOU will save me
I trust YOU, I love YOU, and I need YOU
YOU breathe life into me and would never leave me
I will continue to pray and praise YOU

Find your song..."Speak to my Heart" got me through my dark days... I played this song almost every day on my cassette player at home and at school in the 90's. I played it at lunch with my headphones on. Everyone needs that one song, this is my song that connects me at all times, every time, even through the rough times of watching my brother suffer through cancer, the Lord is always there, just ask for Him to speak to your heart...now find your song

Playlist of the Songs

Speak to My Heart
Take me to the King
Tomorrow / God is Blessing
You Brought the Sunshine / Thank You
Rough Side of the Mountain/ Good & Bad
You Covered Me / How Great Is Our God
The Beauty of the Cross / I Shall Wear a Crown
Just for Me / Restored
Sweet Sweet Sound / God Favored Me
Breakthrough / Go Tell It on the Mountain
Safe in His Arms / We've Come to Worship You
In My Name / For the Rest of My Life
No Greater Love / Oh What Love
Take Me Higher /Trusting and Believing
My Name is Victory /Every Praise
Good God /Church Medley
The Holy Ghost
Let Everything that has Breath Praise
Break Every Chain
Work in your Favor / They That Wait
What Do you Do / Stand
I Smile / God in Me
Stayed on You

Emotions of a Sinner

Love, trust, strength, faith,
Embrace, smiles, laughs, I cry
Disappointment, excitement, delight,
Wrong, right, hope, I cope
Lust, sex, love, weak, strong, wonder, I ponder
Wish, dream, scream, fiend, shake, I wait
Addict, crazy, lazy, procrastinate, chill, I will
Heat, cool, cold, warm, hot, thirst, I work
Talk, listen, hug, kiss, stroke, I spoke
Give, get, loss, choose, bless, rest, I stress
Exposed, naked, fake, truth, open, close, I chose
Time, family, friends, hide,
Deceive, I'm still pleased
Money, honey, up, down, rich, broke, I speak
Reach, swim, walk, run, heaven sent,
Over, under, stretch, I teach
Love is still here, faith, belief, invisible, divisible,
surrounded by HIS arms, my experience
Wrong, right, love in sight, the emotions of my life,
I repent
Pain, Passion, Progress
I survived through courage

Romans 3:23

Culture

As I disconnect from social media on my fast
I focus on my task to build a platform
I want it to be authentic
And genuine with the goal of bridging the gap.
I know a lot of people's faith lacks
Because of the church
We are too focused on the clergy
And the preachers' mixed messages
Instead, we need to focus on God's blessings
Men and women will disappoint you each time
However, our focus should be on the True sublime,
the mighty LORD
So I say focus on the spiritual
And try to live by the principles of HIS love
Christ forgive me for my thoughts on religion,
The rules from that man-made system of it has to be
this or that, reference *Take me to the King*
Baptists and Catholics, so called Christians
Who focus on the practice of rituals
Even though once a week I'm at *Ritual*
Each time I try a different dish,
So I get a variety from the kitchen,
I feel that's worth a mention,
This lets me be flexible about my mission,
Here on Earth I must be prepared
For different ways to deliver
Nourishment for the soul,

Culture continued

Diverse ways of being bold
To help someone with deliverance
Through my testimony, where God gets the glory
That's why I share my stories of how
HE has brought me through,
I am a sinner just like you, no judgements,
When it comes to sin I'm the worst
I could write a book about sin
And for the world it would be the best seller
New York Times,
Getting applause from the young fellas
But I'm here to tell you,
No sin is greater than another
And remember the judgement is
From the physical church
I pray we stay focused on the one and only church,
the only one God governs
There is always a seat available for us
And forgiveness HE lends
And HIS love never ends
So where do we begin, for me it's April Aspirations

Daily

Every Day

Do Something

That gets you

Close to God

Channel your energy to think of the purest thing

That you can do to be more Christ- Like

Practice

Gentleness

Goodness

Faithfulness

Meekness

Self-control

Galatians 5:22-23

The Defining Moment:

Whispering the Word in the World

Or

Be a Bold Christian with a Beautiful Walk

Who will share the good news?

2 Corinthians 3: 11-12

The afterlife of accomplishments on earth, is it possible to be content? Or is it something else to desire? When you think you are finished what was old becomes new again, more of a renewal, or tunnel vision...peaceful talks of how plans have changed or maybe the plans are highlighted in a view that you were not able to see before? I said I was finished writing, but God said you have more to do, more to dream, more to accomplish in My Name. This will take you where I want you to be. Be Bold and step outside the mold and let your light shine, let actions take place, have active faith, let the brand stay in place, the placement of the symbol which creates a conversation, This is who I am, let me embrace...an opportunity to strengthen my witness, the purpose my contribution to the kingdom, in my heart this provides more freedom, another way for me to see HIM...be bolder

Legacy

What name will remain and reign
What is our concern?
Will my name follow for generations?
Will I do something amazing?
Will I Build a legacy to let others know who I am?
Through Wisdom and Patience,
I understand this situation
You must focus on the building blocks to have your name, where it is bright and on display
When HE opens up the Book of life,
The only legacy; eternal life
The streets of gold
With many mansions my achievement

John 14:2

Imagine

Thoughts of how it all works
As I dream through the night
Maybe I am living a dream inside a dream like
"Inception"
This life is really the dream
And when it is time to awake
I will take a supersonic magical escalator ride to
heaven just like the Heavenly Kid
I will have a greeting squad there to cheer me on,
which consists of angels and the people that prayed
for me while I was on Earth...
Then the words "Job Well Done"

And I will see all the choices I made with the Spirit
and the outcomes if I use the spirit,
All in a blink of an eye,
No reason to ask why,
On display is every outcome
And reason of every event,
Every answer if you decided to go right or left,
If you said yes or if you said no...
The meaning of your life...
As I awake from one of the dreams,
What is the meaning of this...

Imagine

(Inspirations: Prayer)

Dear God, grant me the peace in my heart not to worry and lose the need to control. Let me trust in YOU through my actions. Give me the peace in my mind that YOU are working out all of my concerns. I ask for continual covering for my loved ones. Help me to develop the faith that everything will be okay. Let me not focus on what can be seen but focus on the unseen. Thank you for protection and the opportunity to see your signs, miracles and wonders. Continue to mold me in Jesus' Name, Amen.

The List

Make a list of 52 things that are important to you
Ask yourself these questions...
What does my list mainly consist of?
Do I think the list is representing what I want to do
or who I am?
What have I learned about myself?
Have I taken the inward journey
Of knowing myself?
Also, what about my relationship with God?
How many projects have I started
And then lost focus during the year?
What types of things cause me to lose focus?
How important is it for me to accomplish
This project or goal?
Now edit the list of the 52 things....

ABillion Smiles Message

Bible Based, Christ Centered, Prayer Minded
Going straight to the bible for some wisdom
about helping others in Love.

Old Testament
"One who is gracious to a poor man lends to the LORD, And He will repay him for his good deed."
Proverbs 19:17 NASB

New Testament
"But whoever has the world's goods, and sees his brother in need and closes his heart against him, How does the love of God abide in him?"

1 John 3:17 NASB

Pin

As the World goes round and round
And constantly pauses,
We express our love through courage causes.
The Love of the Blood,
The color red displays
That we all need that support, that hug,
That direction which fuels our dreams.
The Blood at Christ's expense,
Your sins that have been rinsed…
Share your Christian Experience
And have courage to go after your passion.
This is more than a pin of fashion.
It's "encouragement" to seek the kingdom first
And all these things will be added…

Luke 12:30-31

Pin

(Inspirations: Prayer)

Dear Lord let everything that has breath praise YOU, we praise YOU for the storms, we praise YOU that we are able to stand on a rock, we praise YOU for Jesus' sacrifice, we praise YOU Jesus, that you came, we pray that YOU teach us more about that name, we praise You for the minister that taught us that saying, we pray for the family, he is absent from the body but we still feel his presence, we praise You for memories, we praise YOU for giving us a new teacher, we praise YOU that our purpose is to stay bible based, Christ centered, as we execute Mathew 4:19, let's do it with contemporary, creative and cutting edge approach, we praise YOU for every breath, now let us give YOU every praise,
In Jesus' Name, Amen

Reflection

Reflection, I seek HIS protection,
Life's lessons, these are my confessions,
Shortcomings of what I was meant to be
Because of my selfish actions,
Too surface, too much concern for fashion,
My focus on looking good and relaxing…
What is my P.O.P life?
Where is the passion, the objective and the purpose
put into action?
Why am I so easily distracted,
It is time to create the magic
With a simple reaction…
Let God lead

Reflection

(Inspirations: Perspective)

What are your Gifts and Talents? What do you think is your purpose for having these gifts? Are you popular for them? How do you use your popularity? What would you do differently now than what you have been doing with your popularity?

For me, popularity helps me to let people see what I can do and to explain my gifts that come from God.

Romans 12:2

Grace, Mercy and Love

Bible Accurate and Christ Bound
Let these words be found as a familiar sound
A beacon of love, an assessment with the Dove
Displaying what is meant from the Heavens above,
The source; our Creator,
Our way maker,
The one and only savior,
The time is now, not later
HE is able to do blessings beyond measure,
The ultimate treasure,
The principle in pleasure,
The unmistakable joy,
The world did not give it,
So the world cannot take it away,
Rooted deep in my foundation… Smile

Grace, Mercy and Love

(Inspirations: Prayer)

No matter the situation....speak to my heart...cleanse my heart, fill it with abundant love, let my heart display Your fruits and goodness...Lord, I need YOU now more than ever...the time is now, to do Your works, YOU are my rock and treasure, let me use my gifts and talents that YOU have given me in a way that displays Your power and glory. Lord, guide me on Your path and show me Your way. Let my heart continue to grow, continue to illuminate my path for a successful journey. In Jesus' Name, Amen

Proverbs 3:5-8   Psalms 51:10

Reflection of Works: The Epilogue

When I wrote Freedom of the Mind, I thought I would release Confessions of Love next, then a book called the Early Years, Where I come from; which is a collection of works from high school and college (so the years would range from 1991-1999)...Then I would finish my catalog with Discovering Devotion in 2007. It took me ten years to release Discovering Devotion and I never released the books that I was going to do. I used the best entries from the book Confessions of Love as a chapter to paint the picture of how I arrived at the Discovering Devotion, which was a vital part of my growth in its release. The collection of my early years' writings I put in the vault and decided there is no reason to release them. All in all my plans have been shifted because they were my plans not God's plans. Once you listen to HIS voice you see clearly your ways are not HIS ways. So book number five is more important to what I am called to do, which you can see from small references in all the previous books. "Inspirations" is my mind and the heart connected to the Source. "God" is the focus on what I should be communicating in my entries. These works are still a journal for me for self-improvement and to show my road toward righteousness. I will never be righteous because I am sinner. However, I can take the road to

Reflection of Works: The Epilogue continued

be the best version God has called me to be. I know there will be plenty of minutes, hours and days that I will constantly be asking for forgiveness as I am human and have shortcomings. My goal is to connect to whatever will help me and others to be closer to God. There is no judgement in my heart, only the boldness to focus on the many mansions. I want us all to get there, but all our paths are different to get there. However, there is only one Source, one airline carrier, one service provider to get you there, which is Jesus Christ...may we all share the good news and achieve eternal life. Let HIS light shine in us and share love.

41

7 the number of completion,
22 forever your birthday and 12 the holy number
7+22+12= 41,
The age you would have been in October,
Now that I'm 41
6 years later… I have 41 reasons to continue to
think what if…
I try to focus on the gift
As I recite poems as if I preach,
The reality is I wrote this for what I seek
In the search of peace, and piece by piece
When I pray in front of the church, I am in relief
Internally I weep for all of the pain I keep
Looking for a way to release
The struggle of your absence
Love is verb, so this is my action
7/22/18 Celebration
James 1: 2, 3, 4 the test, the trials, the tribulations,
The endurance to let the world see my appearance
The Gold Leroy Glow, the Last Dragon
The Secret is Christ's Passion
That is why it never fades
The same yesterday, today, and forever
John 1:1 in the beginning was the Word
And the Word was with God and the Word was God
This is where I start to realize we are never apart
We are all with God if we believe in the Savior

41 continued

You taught me that
When I was young at the dinner table
The key to my foundation, this is my Life I speak,
This body is borrowed
But with Christ, my soul I keep
My words are God driven;
HE blew air in this instrument
Therefore, read my words and hear my voice
That *sweet sweet sound* of praise,
Those 40 years of your life,
Those 40 moments I remember,
Those 40 reasons to dance in September,
Those 40 ways you displayed
Your courage and strength,
Those 40 thoughts of *if I had only known*
How you impacted my life
Those 40 times I wish you were here in the physical
How 41 is divisible by itself
Which is one, and there can only be one you
I still cry on *Once in While*
41 years later, I will still miss you
However, I have 40 and 1 reasons to smile
I know when this circle ends;
You will come back to me again
This is a promise only for a Christ Believer
Join us Acts 2:41

Majestic Forte

The MF Signature

Printed in the United States

www.ingramcontent.com/pod-product-compliance
Lightning Source LLC
Chambersburg PA
CBHW051134160426
43195CB00014B/2463